Your Heart Will Fly Away

DAVID RIGSBEE

Also by David Rigsbee

Poetry:

Stamping Ground (1976)
The Hopper Light (1988)

Limited Editions:

Ratio (1977)
To Be Here (1980)

Critical:

An Answering Music: On the Poetry of Carolyn Kizer (1990)

Anthology:

The Ardis Anthology of New American Poetry (1977)

Your Heart Will Fly Away

DAVID RIGSBEE

The Smith ⊺ Brooklyn

Published by The Smith
69 Joralemon Street, Brooklyn, NY 11201
Typography by Pineland Press
1074 Feylers Corner Road, Waldoboro, ME 04572
Printed at Capital City Press
Box 546, Montpelier, VT 05602

Library of Congress Cataloging-in-Publication Data:
David Rigsbee, 1949 —
Poetry
ISBN: 0-912292-97-0

92-080447 CIP
First Edition, June 1992

Artwork © 1992 by Jim Kay
Author's photo © 1992 by Jim Zietz

Acknowledgments

The poems have previously appeared as follows: "Autobiography," *The New Yorker;* "White" and "The Mermaid," *Poetry;* "The Mountaintop," *Amelia;* "The Trawlers at Montauk," *Crazyhorse;* "Anymore" and "The Word 'World' in Jarrell," *The Denver Quarterly;* "The Rescue," *Florida Review;* "Crickets" and "Sunbathing," *The Georgia Review;* "The River of Becoming," *Hubbub;* "Platonic," *Pembroke Magazine;* "Buried Head," "Collected Poems" and "F-Stop," *Prairie Schooner;* "Secondary Road" and "Stories Away," *The Southern Humanities Review;* "Atomic Future," *The Southern Poetry Review;* "Bermudas," "La Bohème" and "Half-Lives," *The Southern Review;* "Heart and Soul," *Tar River Poetry;* "Lumber," *Three Rivers Poetry Journal;* "Mozart," *Willow Springs.*

These poems have been reprinted as follows: "Crickets," *The 1984 Anthology of Magazine Verse and Yearbook of American Poetry* (Monitor Books), also *The Georgia Review Fortieth Anniversary Retrospective* and in *Keener Sounds: Selected Poetry from The Georgia Review,* edited by Stanley Lindberg and Stephen Corey; "Half-Lives" and "The Mermaid," *The 1987 Anthology of Magazine Verse and Yearbook of American Poetry* (Monitor Books).

The National Endowment for the Arts and the Djerassi Foundation provided creative writing fellowships.

Special thanks to Steven Ford Brown, Roberta Green, Rodger Kamenetz, Carolyn Kizer, and Lloyd Van Brunt.

Contents

3.

1.

Your Heart Will Fly Away

They were playing "Shangri-la" and "It's All in the Game"
from the pavilion bullhorns, and across the street,
in the park, a pipe organ drilled and stuttered its way
through a repertoire of Strauss, its blank angels
and marzipan Alpine figures jerking and circling
through the rococo façade of a German scene.
The loss of its twin during the First World War
only enhanced this wooden contraption, a rasping,
booming, twittering machine, in the slightly out-of-tune
way of player pianos. Old people and kids like us
would watch the angels gibbeted on the tenor pipes
and the Bavarian maid, who threw up her hands
each evening when she sailed on her monorail straight
into the chest of the wooden bully, whose nude legs
were meant to signify his preference for *lederhosen*.

But we tired of this and would mill around the audience,
leaving our seats to Shriners and vets, who came
to the beach glittering with insignia. Better, we thought,
were those new old songs, the adrenaline strains
of the Maguire Sisters and The Platters. We knew
what it meant when smoke got in our eyes, palming
our cigarettes under the pier, or choking in the bathroom,
when the adults left us to sprawl and bake on bare sand.
My uncle, a handsome man with military bearing,
would sit his daughter on his lap and let her swizzle
his beer, taking obvious pleasure in his favoritism.
The shrapnel crease on his cheekbone gave him
the roguish and *savoir-faire* look of a corsair,

and he dismissed the chilly distance of his in-laws
as a breeding fault, and mingled only as duty demanded.

His generation, formed in the war, found themselves
hard by middle-age, the butt of Jimmy Hatlo gags.
Their hairy legs and pointy bras, the wave-pull
of their prejudices: how easy to shove them out of mind!
Germany, Japan, Okinawa, Korea — lunar names,
places that put distance in the voices of the songs we
begged them to turn down, or off, or twirl beyond
until they had reached *our* station, the fast-talking,
put-on DJs we loved and mimicked but didn't understand.
On the beach, they barked like terriers from transistors,
guarding the blankets of bathing beauties. They
said love was a matter of territory: you get some
and hold the rest of the world at arm's length.
But those blankets may as well have been land mines,
for all that we could approach them.

I cruised the boardwalk every day, each hot dog
and fry joint pumping doo-wop into the afternoon,
hoping for anything I could get away with before
returning to the *ennui* of family and my small
place in it. For family seemed merely a concatenation
of chance persons, some sly joke of luck, a ruse
to try the patience that one might someday be in need of.
We were all more or less this way, as though if we
squeezed our eyelids and fists tight and long enough,
we might miraculously disappear from each other's
presence. One of my cousins accosted total strangers,
confessing that he wanted to be a priest; another had
developed the habit of licking his lips so habitually
that the skin flared and we seemed to be talking to
Al Jolson. The adults were even more affected:

One uncle insisted on introducing us to *pizza*.
The prominent false teeth of his wife clicked annoyingly;
as a result, questions to her were peremptory and rare.
Another had put a mesh over the grille of his Cadillac
and gave us minute tours of the entomological treats.
The ocean shimmered, meanwhile, and we fell
into its rhythm, while the pipe organ swelled and whined
and the rock music boomed. How was I to know
a current deeper than any bass was the real wave
we surged on? How can I forgive myself that ignorance,
except as part of a massive forgiveness for all that time
would offer to any stubborn and hungry being?
Even then, the heaviest, most secret of waves
was lifting us into its motion, as we snapped our suits
and bored each other with transparent *braggadocio*.

The Bavarian maid and the wooden bully entertained
the veterans night after night, as did other antics
on the organ's face. Cruisers and would-be Lotharios
jammed the streets in their Impalas and Fairlanes,
heads bobbing in the ecstasy of their radios: *You have
words with him, and your future's looking dim.*
But the future didn't look that way, except in a song.
Rather, with quick centrifugal force, we felt
the present circling, hurtling with us in it, toward
a piece of time that was ours alone, that was freedom
and grace and the ease of our aunts and uncles,
were they only to realize that was what they had.
Yet it seemed that they didn't know. How else explain
their tawdry interests, their inability to appreciate
the line we clutched to our imaginations: *and your*

heart will fly away? Of course it would, in the stealth
of night, after my cousin's too-fervent prayers, after

the other had rubbed down his lips with Vaseline:
then I dropped from the window and stole to the beach
where the Major's daughter, my cousin, waited under
a jaundiced moon, where the sand drummed with crabs
and the surf arrived importantly, then died as froth.
There she lifted her shirt and pointing to her breasts said,
"These will be big someday, you know." I knew
something, though I forget the rest of our chatter.
We lay head-to-head and faced the stars till dawn,
listening to the all-night radio, the promises saturated
with tenderness: *And when you hold me, how warm
you are.* But we had held nothing except the words,
which would one day weigh less than a breath.

And there was something else: we did rise
in time, some *above,* some *away.* That was also
the meaning of the organ that sailed over, the war
before the war. What else could it have been saying but
Remember me, I was someone's once, now I am yours?
I forgive it for having said so, if that is what it said.
Today I stop at a curb, and a swan-necked girl in a Porsche
waits for me to cross, and when I reach the opposite curb,
she accelerates theatrically, as if to make her mood
obvious. There's some rap music spilling from
the cockpit, and I think, *I like that too,* as though
nothing else were ever as eager to put its diamond stylus
against us and play a soundtrack for the rest of time.
She laughs over the waves of traffic, and I am tender
meat still for the sun to broil. I throw up my hands.

The Mountaintop

At the top of the mountain
I sit down by a rattlesnake skin
blowing like a windsock

on a stalk of dry grass
whose leaves
chirr in the bluster.

The whole mountaintop shimmers
and the eye moves beyond
to the hills' stabilities

and beyond that to the ocean,
where cloud-bands
level in even with the shoreline.

Above it, the light, dusty blue,
darkens toward the zenith
into a seemingly more acute

complexity.
Forty now, I hear
in the dry ratchetings

faint, repeated allusions
to other stories and times
briefly touching this one.

What matter? It's the climb
I'm after to the Wordsworthian
purview and the sublimity.

The flies buzz about.
I skim them off my clothes
like some old horsetail.

Quietly, it occurs to me,
with the range of hills
undulating in stillness to the edge of sight,

how naturally
and with what vigorous ease
the flies have flown to the mountaintop.

Buried Head

A bumblebee strafes the aged gold mines.
In the garden, magnificent rot: tomatoes eviscerated,
hanging like bags; sunflowers that were once
bright pies on stakes, bend and crook into canes.
In the fields, stopped wheels of hay, implying journey,
clutter before the horizon, above which
battalions of clouds roll up and forward,
implying the end of happiness, if this is what happiness

has been. I drag wood from the garden pile,
careful of the snakes who occasionally
slither in to make life miserable. It will be
a lovely, tinderbox fire, the kind one would expect
of a phoenix. Whereas in fact, these stacked
combustibles were recently the joists and structure
of an old massive wing, until a tornado
arrived one day and quickly settled their hash.

Stick by stick, I will feed the house to itself,
as I have cannibalized myself to make
the fire brighter. Up through the chimney
and into the atmosphere from which one might
spot other lights and other fires in preparation
for future engagements. Afternoon drags
through the yard like an old dog, beside which
cars flash down the highway into town.

Following one, spring-loaded with kids, my eye
stops at the bronze head, half-buried in the grass.

Its wind-washed face tilts toward the porch
where I sit. It's surrounded by chaos, weeds,
and broken pottery that have given up any sense
of relationship to the world, whose rhythm
is above all relentless, be it broken down
by forgotten seasons or Sahara-wide minutes.

Some sparrows assemble on a wire that awaits
a voice to prove geography a simple joke.
(And if geography, why not time?) One darts
away over the firehouse. Tonight's freeze
will strangle the mist of gnats that floats
at the screen and supersede all this
buzzing and yellowness. Suddenly, nothing
 will seem so important as getting up half-frozen

just to see the sight of that gun-metal hair.

Crickets

They are without memory, making
up the night's story continually,
like Scheherazade. They are the old men
who pull the wool caps down
over their brows after the fashion
of railway baggage clerks.
They limp, paying no mind
to a missing leg. They crawl
in the bottom of bait buckets
knowing there is no exit.
When the grass grows thick
as the pile of a Persian rug,
and intoxicated with rain,
bully with heat, they are there
picking their way through tropical
forests. Then when night comes
and with it desire, and with it
love, and with it love's decline,
and with it death and the second death,
they take their place in the orchestra.

Atomic Future

My father returns from his garden
to his chair. He is worried about me,
recalling the specter of unemployment
and the old tyranny of debt. He worries
too about his legs, bum now, the veins
long since pulled out like squash webbing.
Legs that must still propel him daily
to his dried-out bean rows and back.
To the deck, den, stairs, and thence
to bed. Like me, he has no other choice

but to make it work, whatever "it" is.
He flips open a copy of *Omni* and reads:
"Atoms will rotate around each other for
the universe's lifetime without showing wear."
Sounds that emerge this fall evening,
as if no longer toggled to bodies, spread forward:
children's shouts mix with the staccato
barking of the smaller, more paranoid dogs,
which in turn connects with the bug Muzak.
Finally, like an afterthought, a jet

somewhere moles upward through clouds,
routinely transcending the sky cover.
Perhaps he *should* worry. After all, I'm
those same atoms reconfigured into this self,
spinning exactly to the end of my lifetime.
But first I have to figure out the cash-
flow problem and afterward superimpose

the "what-if?" scenarios of the next
few months onto my worry screen
like the transparent overlays that build

a frog in a child's encyclopedia. I think
of him taking extra jobs, when my mother
would silently place the pot roast down
on the trivet, exhorting us, with a look, to eat.
Now retired, he delves into the structure
of atoms and stages in the lives of the galaxies,
meanwhile worrying about the stages
of my checking account. He reads on:
"They will clasp each other with the exact
same degree of force forever." The beans,

stunted and desiccated by drought,
hang like an old pianist's arthritic fingers.
All summer his tiller raised nothing
so much as golden dust. Still he stands
by the dry bed of the garden, at the white
string rectangle that outlines its promise.
He is like a madcap football coach inventing
razzle-dazzle plays to save a victory,
though the players and fans have long
since disappeared down the maw of time.

I will have to do some fancy footwork soon.
That's clear. And I know there's some further
humiliation waiting. I can sense the remote,
patronizing gaze bearing down like faint
starlight from the end of the Milky Way,
arriving in time to catch my father dozing
off in his chair. It will hang like vapor fuzz
on the skylight until the zodiac drags it off.

For that, I will gradually grow a carapace,
or find more pity in the flesh, I don't know.

The evening's heavy sonic wave becomes
the night surf. Somewhere upon that relay
is a voice trying to get through to explain
about the bonds holding matter together.
I'm ready to record that message and store
it in the same memory-register where
my father is arriving from the night shift.
He places his black empty lunch pail
on the table. He's been loading boxes
onto trailer trucks, and his legs are stiff.

I see his fingers wrap around the door
as he looks in on us, his face obscured
by the light behind him. Because I'm broke
I don't want that memory to have to live
by itself anymore. He scrapes together some
leftovers, perhaps spaghetti, or a pimento
cheese sandwich my mother has left out.
We hear him moving about the kitchen
for hours, postponing minute by minute
the sleep that will stop his legs for a while.

Lumber

The jet drags its belittling roar
across the hills, and the thought
occurs to me: *the violence isn't fury,*
the spectacular desire for elsewhere.
No triumphal feeling attaches to it,
only burning, blinkered industry.
Its escaping aluminum glint
decorates the azure like the flash
of a gold tooth during the course
of a joke. Better that we tumble,
I say, like spent pods from a weed,
released from their pinched destinies
to learn the ground is unconfining,
as though they willed it so,
as against so many rooted, godlike
postures of the trees — their apotheosis —
lost forever in their thickets and woods,
just ground cover, just lumber.

La Bohème

Someone said it was like country music.
It was clear what she meant, the way it gets
hooks into you faster than you can protect yourself.
And close to life, too, as when you peel away
the layers of interference: clothes thick and ill-
fitting, the zest with which the hero's roommates
approve the existential echoes of each other's banter,
while furtively observing her from the corners
of their slum. Still, it's the way it happens
there in the dark: love's expiring air, reeling
out a sumptuous music as it goes — and dawn
rising to contrast the poverty of the whole thing,
absorbing stars as the scene changes. Conveyor-
belt silhouettes glide by outside, indifferent
and unconcerned with the fat girl everyone's
made such a fuss about. Just like country music.
You know you should get up, make your way
past the warm knees to the lighted runway,
following whatever threads of pride you still have left.
But you stay, letting it happen, convincing yourself
of its significance, as she, leaning up from her deathbed,
cuts loose and goes straight for the last-row hearts.
And you sit back while the endless swan song drills
your sternum as if it were a rock, against every instinct
that could have meant something more dignified,
before the death and the pity started,
before it all got so terribly out of hand.

The Rescue

Sun shifts. Our shadows long as the blues.
Night is a rescue, everyone's OK.
The groundhog beetles along the fence,
his skin loose: he is the dollar-bill
inside a purse. Other things are in
the grass. They crisscross, avoiding
contact like Giacometti figures.
Night will slide forward like a convertible
top, and we'll go riding, but this time
no cruising, no demands on the mind.
No wind-up manias for the dawn
to scrape away. A beetle hogs the porchlight.
When he makes a pass, he stirs
the other bugs in his wake: none of that.
I wouldn't even boss words around,
except I want to get on with it,
the blues fading and then the rescue.

The River of Becoming

> The leaves peel
> back: there the raisin-sized
> buds — whole warty branches waving,
> drinking light,
> more lived-through than new,
> yet more accomplished
> than a virtuoso.

When you held the infant up, bobbing
in the nearly palpable round of her sleep, the world
was a far country the mind simply files away.
Did someone once encircle my whole body so,
as though miming the *lacrimae rerum*,
as the philosopher threw his arms around
the whipped horse, crying, "O my brother!"?
Did I, in infancy, treat with incipient contempt
what was heard only as a disturbance?

A calf dropped and lay in the pasture for days,
a breach birth, its mother unable, too much bother
for the farmer, who marked it for veal.
Starlight and the confusing shadows of the herd
coming and going along the river path
inched across the wet marble of its eye.

> There exists a moment
> like that between night and morning
> when something unheard of
> is brought forward to be

handed off
to its successor: time pauses
at the connection, can be said
not to be.
Words, like blown smoke,
pursue the moment.

Could those I declined still have voice
        to tell me their fears from the edge
of my cast-off days? Could perhaps still others
        relay their messages in the valleys
between words of an ordinary exchange;
        or the domestic scream
halt in a siding in order to let the silence pass
        like a train filled with suits and papers?

The calf was rescued by passing joggers
who had noticed a dark spot on a little rise
outside the shade of a pine,
about which the herd clustered and went.

Then the corridor is bare.

        But the house is cluttered: the litter of thought.
Even a fortune, escaped from its cookie,
        lies on the rug as if in motion, arrested
on the way to promote its sentence to prophecy.
        All is jockeying through the layers
for a bit of the next life,
        not less than a thousand photographs
of cancelled arrangements, all ready-to-hand.

Waxwork tulips raise their cups
to the highway.

> *Are they the truths these leave-takings*
> > *are the flying transformations*
> *of? Filled with what tender nothings?*
> > *What radiance in the crumbling*
> > > *bowls?*

The family omits to mention. The children
run room to room by the obvious
    that also quickens my steps. The sound
of their voices that for the moment are
    the arrows of time streaming from their quiver,
become the string shuddering to rest.

Outside, a string of vines
sets forth its digression-less agenda.

> > *The runners go up*
> > > *the hill*
> > > *beside the electric fence;*
> > *they go down and you*
> *don't see them again but notice*
> > *the pasture darkening to*
> > > *a pastoral brown.*

You saw the veins of that baby's sleeping skull:
the red sapling in her bare white head
    there in the hallway, like the tree of earth's
continuation and renewal, tree of the body's knowledge
    and its passing that was continually offered
and continually refused.

> *And what trees have you let stand,*
> > *what shade brought to the summer*
> > *things, quisling Other?*

The river of becoming has shrunk
          from its banks, and it is only
     spring, only the mechanism
               of lost seasons,
and the brown spread
          of returning ground
     that draws me to it.

2.

Heart and Soul

The life that is not here calls up.
What do you want, I say.
I want you to come with me, it says.

We have some unfinished business,
some supplements and additions,
some moments of truth unaccounted for.

That's fine with me, I say.
I want nothing but the truth,
though, to be frank,

I don't want the truth
to be a fetish, either. The life
that is not here is silent for a moment.

Well then, come on, it says,
I'll be waiting for you. It hangs up
but instead of a dial tone

there's marimba music:
an exotic rendition of "Heart and Soul."
I recognize it at once.

So that was what it was,
I say to myself, and to think
it waited all this time.

Mozart

I had a fantasy about size,
that we were all terribly small
in the field of each other's memories.
That we were scattered and subject
to the direst revisions.

Naturally I want to be whole
again, as in childhood,
and the proper size for thinking
about. But again is a fantasy too
when you think about it.
There are no agains, only approximate
repetitions we say hello to
as if greeting acquaintances at work.
Pretty soon the trenches get rearranged,
and then where are we?

From this distance the cows are brushstrokes.
They should thank God for filing
them under the dumb animals.
After a while they become dots,
then just a smell as they graze
toward the farther pasture, just
something that passes through the nose
like dust through a screen.

My house is in reality a *gemütlich*
little rattrap, and this a rat's lyric,
the wind that only tractors ahead,

eliminating, by way of passing,
both music and the Muses.
I wish that it were a white mansion,
and that there were a man walking
through, his sweet limbs swinging
as he held the heel of a violin
against his jugular. Because
of all the notes, there must be one
resolution, a signature, that can make
a wedge into the eventual silence,
like the vanishing point in a landscape,
and that one note, like the silence,
he wouldn't play.

F-Stop

My neighbor's horizontal back moves
beyond her shrubbery like a floating island.
She's weeding the space in front of the bushes,
her eyes as flawless and dispassionate
as a quality control expert's.

The light too is growing horizontal
as the sun makes its way down among
the impediments of trees and houses
like an old gentleman descending
bleacher steps in the bottom of the eighth.
He knows the game is over already.
You don't have to paint him a picture

or try his patience with extraordinary accounts
of hope. And yet the front-yard leaves
have become translucent, which means
the passage of light through matter and out
the other side, creating filtered pools and oblongs
that stand inside the overhangs
an F-stop higher than shade.

Perhaps I should go and speak to her,
though the preliminaries deny easy access
to conversation's give-and-take.
And after all, she is about the business
of setting her grounds in order
in spite of the imminence of fall.

She plucks the fugitive, early brown
leaves along with the weeds,
in motions so pleasingly negative
(though I can't see them) that
she seems in some respect to slow time
simply by her brisk, praiseworthy labor.

Now the sun, settling onto a roof,
paints my wall with a frame
of straight-on light and an exact shadow
of the glass door-bars.
It inches across the wall toward
the hall door, dimming as it goes
until I can't see it, and as a result
never enters. The porpoise of her
back continues to swim beyond
the bushes as evening arrives.
In the distance, the stadium lights
apply their chilly brilliance.

There's something there I'm not seeing,
something she can't quit and go inside for,
nor I come out to find her sunken face
puttering into the cool, pleasant evening.
Which is why I don't speak to her:
we can't see eye to eye.

The Word "World" in Jarrell

If I think about it, I get lost when I see
a new slab put into place. What was yesterday
ground is now foundation, and arriving for
their constitutionals, the mockingbirds blench.
Construction cranes transform the air
into boxes of itself. Will I alone
be the unchanged one? Who am, myself,
a long box of echoes? If I don't get
the words right, the new library
rises in spite of me. This means
more explaining on my part, like a baker
who's stopped to sneeze, and the loaves
back up. Damaged, I'll nonetheless lean
to the thing that's moving beyond me.

The long waveform of the oak branches:
I used to walk by here on my way to work,
and the stylish trilling of the birds
followed exactly the predictable bird-
language of Heraclitus. Now deflected
from this square of world, their songs
struggle against the straitjacket of their
occasions, and I'm no longer sure, among
so many unsettling givens, what the debate
is still about, or that debate at all
describes what this contention really is.
Once I stood by Jarrell's grave and smelled
the boxwoods sweetening the field, the same
shrubs that had sweetened my childhood.

And I remembered that a *Fragment* describes
how, in Hades, souls perceive by smelling,
as the flow of past life is jarred loose
in spring. Structurally speaking, the slab
and a bookshelf are identical. How sad,
then, to seed the books with the word
"world," as if one brought the other
into being by will or necromantic power;
or book were to life as "world" is to this
shifting habitation. Instead, the birds
are dabs of pathos, and songs lean automatically
toward their shelves. Already I have to go
a new way to work, and things, I know,
are not going to be so easy as they once were.

Autobiography

As soon as you leave, you enter
memory, and that small emissary
of yourself immediately loses
its credentials. No longer yours,
you can't recall it, or send it
instructions on tactical lying.
You may have armed yourself with
heavy qualifiers, been Henry James,
but turn your back, it's theirs.

Thus, memory. And each fresh
installment of yourself, though
exquisite, is still lump clay.
Even the other tack, sincerity,
has zero chance because revelations
have nothing to do with memory.
Trapped, you have only the whim
they toss at you to put on.
You are a small being now, just

a fraction of the old self.
Your mother tongue begins to suffer,
like an émigré's. Plainly, you
were the aggregate of what you gave
up. Now you are suspiciously
plural. What is happening to you?
It is like glimpsing someone who
favors you in an old movie
you used to like. And yet,

the costume is absurd, not to
mention the horse. Or these
others, also with your face, jerk-
ing their spears in the air.
Spilled change, their faces turn
briefly to the you they obviously
can't see. And the barbaric
shouts they make, this cast of
thousands swarming over the dust!

God's Tumbler

What perishes will reappear

as the clouds come
gathering our shadows
and giving them back again.

From the pool I looked out
and saw the green
launched out of the earth

behind the lying bodies.
What a green it was,
and no one, I thought,

had ever seen it so.
A helicopter flew over
and then a bird whose

mysterious purpose seemed nonetheless
apt. But the foundation of this
building where my life ripened

into today
became something else
as I looked down.

Suspended, it might well
have levitated
were it not as

dependent as anyone could make it.
I wished then that
somebody had been around

to applaud and corroborate
this Wallenda-esque, high-wire
fact of gravity

that dangled the building
before me like a splendid
joke, if only because

it seemed it *could* have come unhooked
and fallen, against reason,
into sheer air.

The proximity of that
chaos brought you, my friend,
to mind,

and nothing moved,
as I could imagine it moving
but stayed firmly in place.

A little tumbler —
so the legend goes —
when asked to produce his offering

at the Virgin's shrine
stood directly and at length
on his head

to the amazement of
his pious colleagues who were
further astounded

by the laughing Queen
and company of Heaven
suddenly in their midst.

Even from that perspective
he must have seen both
the emptiness under his feet

and the inverted figure
of himself, which had to make do
with the merest tissue

of being when the vision
was gone.
The trembling of foundations

is any man's fear,
an undistributed middle term
that the mind seizes on

in its mania
for survival.
Meanwhile, the birds

sing out of the green,
make nests,
and do not stare at their wings.

So in the reflected world,
washed and moving
like the water itself,

I imagined you again,
who reminded me of the willing acrobat.
And you were alive for me

whom I had thought dead.
But what perishes
reappears

according to a primordial plan
whose existence I learned of
reading a book

I had opened casually
beside the water
of a swimming pool.

And was implicated
by memory and emptiness
in its simpler,

perfected longing.

Sunbathing

Something in each of these bodies
will never happen again.
And so they situate themselves
around the pool, as if the streams
of light will mean
it was finally all right to be
a secret, like the torsos of cherubs
with chunks torn out of the backs.

The older lie in a different way,
sometimes turning awkwardly on their sides
as the young would never do.
It is a posture for regret,
poising that way as if
the earth were closer, and they
carrying a burden more physical,
whereas they are actually

emptier. Lying around this
rectangle that precisely reflects
the undeviating blue, they
simulate sleep, if they are not
sleeping, and this is as true
as it gets in the sun,
a few hours of meanwhile,
and the night tilting upward.

Stories Away

Many stories go around the table:
there's the story of the Zurich
junkies, the parks trashed out with syringes;
the story of the pit-bull muggers
roaming Central Park;
the one about Mick Jagger
coming into the restaurant with one of his
anorexic beauties
and staring worriedly, silently at
the sconces all night long.

The piled plates are congealed.
Someone serves "ginger tea."

Suddenly there's a thud at the screen
and somebody shouts, "Look!"
The old cat's left a headless hare
at the door, gross and pathetic,
grotesquely streamlined like in a grocery store,
but still beautiful, still made for flight.

And beyond the deck rail, the moon
hooking the mountain as it sets
and the stars brightening gradually,
even the faint ones for which
there are no violins, no pianos
tinkling over the lake.

Platonic

At least the singing creatures have their
poise between them, while we lie down
and fade into the dreams we earned.

How tired even the lamps look, as though
the illuminations were just some lazy rain
from the shades onto what we now ignore:

books and clocks, plants held captive in their
imported soil. Bits of outdoor light, nailed
to porches and meant to organize darkness

are apt to fool only bugs. And so
the dog tags jangle around the dog's neck
as he swings his heavy muzzle around,

convinced that something will arrive through
the dark air, of which he is guardian
and why we keep him under the house.

His rustling and occasional snuffle
are responses to whole zones
of the grass, swarming with the congenial

night. And the river is itself a noiseless
dark on whose shores the shacks and houses
sit without particular meaning,

artifacts lost forever in a cave where
great bears stride easily along the floor
toward light, not having a use for tools.

The Mermaid

Both freshly divorced,
my brother and I met at the shore
for the brief solace of a holiday.

His eyes still sparkled
as he reeled in a twisting, liver-colored
shark and, wedging it

underfoot, carefully removed
the thin steel hook that pierced the lip,
then kicked it back into the sea

as the pier crowd looked on.
"You can see all kinds of things
if you stay out long enough,"

he explained, "and you have
enough beer." His son romped along
the planked surface that seemed,

at night, to stretch aspiringly
over the water, whereas we recognized
its incompletion: it was just

another failed bridge.
Watching the boy, I remembered
the times his father rode

on my shoulders up ravines, through
thickets of ragweed, timothy and cinquefoil
looking for the secret places

of our myth, where no one could find us.
We knew that these places — the hollows,
the dark stands of poplar,

the blackberry brambles —
were ours to be lost in and that
no harm could come to us

there. His son would dream
that privacy too, drifting to sleep
in his pallet above the waves.

Later, fished-out, we looked in
on the island's one immemorial hangout,
a bar called The Mermaid.

Sliding into our booth we watched
the dancers bob and drift to the beery
crooning of a cowboy band.

Bathetic and wistful, but at the same time
entranced, they enacted the forward-looking
poses of love, that old addiction,

whose conclusion, later and far
out into the night, the many nights,
had always equaled, for us, defeat.

As the couples loomed by,
arms looped like block and tackle,
I asked my brother, "Would you

do the same thing over again?
I mean knowing what you know now."
My question issued from

a fictional innocence, like those places
we'd forgotten, yet managed to carry in some
remote store of memory

that now suddenly emerged
into focus with the nostalgic help
of alcohol and desperate music.

He looked out onto the floor
and said nothing for a long time,
two or three songs at least,

two or three stories, any of which
would do to swell the pedal of his own.
Then swung back around

and breaking into a smile,
said, "Of course! Wouldn't *you?*"
With the keeper's sincerity, I said

yes, my answer carrying him
again to a place where all possibilities
contained every future at once,

where girls lured boys
into the blissful, rocking sea of their arms
and all distances vanished

in the zero of a mouth.
For without doubt this was our fraternity too,
to become entangled in the bright

dream of women, moth-drawn, shriveled
with a thousand hungers so that our defeat
became the sacred ground

of a *future* memory. And thoughts
of those cul-de-sacs now beyond reach
were not true memories at all

but empty scrub and bracketed
bare ground incapable of being restored.
What our parents knew

we took, destroyed, and so failed
them, as we failed the others when, through
the intimate bridge of their looks,

we saw the pier-end,
the ocean heave with fabulous fish
and we were not satisfied.

Now, we rose well before closing
and made our heavy ways to the door.
We knew what was in store,

what the dry socket of the moon,
floating in its chill bed, had made fantastic
in us. But tonight we only walked

back to the sleeping child, with the sea
grinding, the frogs exultant, and paused there
in the road to give the couples

the doubtful benefit of a smile,
the lunatic couples propped by their trucks
under the sign of The Mermaid.

3.

Bermudas

You don't honestly think this
    a retreat. The clouds
puff into cones, but you resist
the summarizing impulse which,
    for others, reiterates
a sense of well-being. Here

  you are marginal. The sun finds
    everything out, exposing the air
to every kind of division. There's Spain,
like longing, where the sun has been,
    like the end of life, sitting at the end
of waves, or the truth

  that lies at the end of deception.
    The sound of a power-
saw and lumber stacking: even
in the stress of confinement
    they're finding ways to elaborate
the theme of a respite.

To you it is a ratio, what a life
    would be, reborn as geography.
Overhead, jumbo jets stuffed
with tourists flicker between clouds.
    It doesn't matter that this
indifferent competition of bodies

jades the green body of the island.
        Beyond the golf carts,
    the ocean lifts its glass shoulders.
Behind, the houses
        in their white hats lie frozen
    on the hillsides. If you

    had such a house, anchored at sea,
        jutting into the massive,
    mystifying figures of clouds,
would you know that you were also
        moving? That your house
    belonged also to the fly-away

clouds? True, there is little comfort,
        but what it would have meant
    is not, in any case, clear. These pines
prickle at the rock's edge,
        and below, the froth slips up the sand.
    You are in the middle

    of your life, and because there is
        no rest for the currents,
    no end to the shores and limits,
it is not enough to be
        in the middle of things that
    require a human's certifying gesture.

    A sail's isosceles white,
        with a black "35," like the price
    snipped out of a book, tips
against the horizon.
        The sailors, though busy, wave
    at anybody. But you

turn, enduring the reductive
    confidence of their going,
which, with each cheerful goodbye,
throws its shadow like the net it is,
    while they shrink, yawing and listing
in their tiny boat.

White

The computer screen glows
with the mild indifference
of a new spring day. It is my
substitute for the cerulean
that I bring forward into night.
It serves like a Death's Head
to an Enlightenment dandy.
It covers "what-is-the-case"
like Sherwin Williams.

Midnight. The crystalline
laughter from the apartment
above has become more
intermittent and threatens
to subside altogether, as if
it had surrendered to the rain,
the tapping no one turns for,
to see, at any rate, nothing
but the courtyard birdbath.

Whose dumb angel does not
prevent me from reading:
"In the wisdom of my failure,
I will carry even the last agony
to the grid of meaning."
I mean to paste these lines
to the artificial sky, to fill
its memory screen for a time,
while I sit back, as objective,

as anonymous as snow.
No longer the nosy curator
of my own dusty museum,
I have become philosophical.
Each reduction enriches me
like a quarry into which
the weather loves to come:
the snow of tradition, the rain
of knowledge, all one there.

I hear the laughter again.
Meanwhile, the cats stretch,
yawn, and make biscuits
with their paws. I think
of how love came and ended,
two storms, and yet I retained
my pronoun like a prize-
fighter his unwearable belt.
I drag this thought to the grid.

The screen, thanks to my human
snow, is becoming the brightest
light in the room. I will lend
myself to its blessed storm
until its growing white folds
into the general memory of
what was, that other storm
I sought shelter from, that rolls
like a wave through the world.

The Trawlers at Montauk

Because happiness takes a tremendous
toll, the fisherman's joy gasps
in the greasy hold, just as lovers suck
the surrounding air nearly to a vacuum.

And yet, one's life lumbers by
like a trawler, torn, top-heavy.
"Built by greed," says the ocean.
"Buoyed by hunger," say the nets.

The boats can't stay in one place.
You look again, and they've turned
to the horizon. Soon they are
almost nothing, who killed many fish.

And the sky rises alive from the ocean.
Dr. Chekhov said that men with hammers
should shadow us always, reminding us
of our unhappiness — a thought

bright with moral charm but likewise,
and finally, dark. It would require
a parallel universe, and in time they
would lay down their hammers, exhausted,

and appear, hands outstretched,
mouths open, asking the same pittance
we had always taken for granted
in the soft voice, where hunger begins.

Secondary Road

Coming home in the curdling traffic
on an errand remote from my life,
turning the radio dial aimlessly,
I came upon the *Liebestod,* of all things,
right where the freeway grades into my
secondary road. With that, the first sweet airs
of another summer rushed in,

which I'd forgotten. Or stretched beyond
memory of the swells of throes,
the inconsolable, world-excluding drama
of the self. Now, sealed in my car,
hurtling over the small hills and through linked,
endless fields of corn, I felt that shuddering
overtake me again

and for a few minutes the mystery of it
held on and threw me back: that lacerating thrill,
that death to reach a star . . .
But more charitably, my wonder,
as the sky darkened to evening, and I drove
through the country alone, streaked clouds above,
everywhere the thickening leaves.

Anymore

Something has suddenly ended.
Maybe the cat looks up coincidentally.
Maybe she stares her dream of the world
outward into the room, or maybe
I do.

But something is over and done with.
It's become fact, or maybe history.
Or it travels wobbling into oblivion
where it's whole at last.

The empty wine bottles have candles in them,
and someone's moved who once
ate a meal. The clock strikes three
as though it were only that,
without antecedents, and just as suddenly
it tells a different story.

Something has ended, and the air
keeps coming out of the fan.
The songs of the crickets: what were they
in my father's childhood?
What was the color blue
in his sky-blue eyes?

The river could just about take me
where I want to go, only

another would arrive and be greeted
by strangers, accept their compliments,
endure their nostalgia, and so forth.

One should wear snow shoes
so as not to fall through the world.
This is an after-song, the color blue,
and a cricket: for something has gone down
like a cat from the shelf.
And something has ended
and won't come back anymore.

Tedious Vigil

The German shepherd next door
paces back and forth in his trench.
With the new neighbor installed
on this transient street, his dog's
right to guard against our famous
wanderlust. I get in my car

and whistle to him as I pull out.
He runs the fence, and my pleasantries
to him are as profound as language
to me. For I want this paper,
having poked through, to begin
standing on its curvy stalk

and the congenital strangeness
of its appearance to drop away.
I'm exhausted by this heated mob
of days and afraid that my largesse
of wasted time, my bee-and-flower
thinking, will land me among weeds.

What if the phone rang and a voice
offered me the past? Or I shed my skin
and walked off in my star-white bones?
I buy off the gray, militaristic dog.
I eat a meal as the sun goes down.
Surely this penchant for singing

after broken things is pathological.
What intrigues me is how the books
lie, like fatal stones on the shelf.
What scares me is the guard dog's
tedious vigil. My cat, unimpressed,
parades equally by the real flowers

and the paper ones. Her window
puts her life on the square, while
another window opens to reveal
possibilities for someone else.
What difference, then, that the time
lifts off like a great blue heron

before the ordinary ellipse of my face?

Collected Poems

The telltale spoors
under the jacket-flap of this
big book, this lifework,
hint more loudly of it than
the plain printer's box of
the obituary page, the names
lying down to rest at last
within their little squares.

Slowly, nature erases culture
and life streams through the window
invisibly, in spite of gravity.
So the train's solemn double horn
gives out a double meaning
as it strains down the rusty track
under the Mississippi bridge.
I can take it, or if I can't

I don't want to be the final
mention of my attempts when I am
less spine than this.
I don't want to be the first whisper,
either, of the error I will be
when I lie in memory of such
a river, replaced by spoors
drifting down from the dark waters.

Half-Lives

I watch a chameleon leap
from a fence and snap up a pair
of love bugs, joined, moving sideways
by my feet. They say the female
is most disordered by the male's
collision as he gashes in,
cranes her around, and drifts off like
a speck of soot from a wood blaze.
Yet who believes such old hearsay?
The air over the parking lot's
filled with them and their black shells mashed
into windshields. I set the chaise
back, and watch the purple sky boil
in the south over some green
woods. Now there isn't anyone
by the pool. The aluminum
umbrellas tilt their disks at clouds.
And the smell of rain, as I knew
it would, sends the small lizard back
to his bush. The book I am no
longer reading nevertheless
offers the sentence, "They were twins."
to the perfect reader of such puzzles.
The first drops hit the page,
and I think of the half-lives I
was party to. Tchaikovskian,
unwilling to allow the slant
of thought, the storm drives in full-blown.
I gather the book to my chest

and walk home by the bulb-lit pool.
In the rain, I do not know if
the dark still matters now, or what
I still hold against my heart.

Sequential Views

for Robbert Flick

1.
Horse on a hill. Great bright days
of unspecified emptiness.
The natural world and one in it.

It's nevertheless becoming clearer
just how hard it will be
to do this. You lift the headset

from your hot skull just in time
to catch a chopper or jet
somewhere above the snaking trail

where, as on a walking tour from the last
century, images give way to reflection,
where land is land, primordially rich,

indifferently dispensing and conserving
the horse, the trees, the maniacal flight
of this season's fly, the barnstorming birds,

both swallow and hawk, whose parabolas
make the hills' outlines exponential.
Who will there be to make this reflection,

to measure this land against her own
revisionist cityscape, each successive layer
less and less the length of a generation?

The country dozes in the parentheses
of its headphones, its nostalgias fallen
in the valleys of the beat, no perspective

without what seizes the ear, moment
by moment, the anonymous rattle of long grass,
the bird-cry and wing-swoop going unremarked

like the chatter of idiots, each with a beatitude,
each intoning his peculiar destiny: Milton,
Christ, etc., to a room of similar idiots.

2.
The eye's snapshot takes it: the horse
on the plateau, its neck evolved to an attitude
of curiosity, extended, positioning the soft nose

to inquire of the grasses. For an hour
it will not move, except for the *punka* tail
exercising the flies. You blink, take in

the rest of the field: soft as felt
but for scrub spreading up the valleys
and the occasional inviting tree

that says to the eye, "Come closer,
find the eyes that come back at you,
that you saw in the headlights but

couldn't flush," that burned in the rows
of needles, in the fabled, flame-like trees
that swell in the dark and shrink at morning,

like respiration. You would say the hills
are sleeping, their angularities as soft
as human life. Arrested in their vertical

protrusion, scaled by wind, they offer
instead a various spectacle and variations
on the horizontal theme,

reverie's angle, which holds
some of darkness hostage, even
on a cloudless day and throws busy-ness

and all upstanding thought into farcical
relief. So then, no scheming penetrates
what this landscape is about.

The tiny horse bends to the ground.
At this distance there's no way to know
which end points east, which west.

3.
Socked in with fog, the grass up close,
like a picture. Last night the most outrageous
shrieks, and this morning the brindled cat

donates his dish to jays. I let the old thing,
full of bumps and dings, maunder
into my lap, and then I pick

the thistles from his fur. He returns the gift
of his relaxation and treats me to a bird's-eye
view of his guilty bath.

4.
The fog bank creeps over the hills one by one,
fog of secrets and whispered disclosures,
and the wind picks up: a hawk

lazes into the turbulence. There is sun enough
still for thoughts to go wandering
among grasses and rills, whatever

the earth serves up. I have watched the swallows'
dalliance, a double-dance that translates,
simply, to vertigo. Why so hard to hold

their moving spiral in the mind? — except
that its formal nuances offend emotion,
while the mind takes stock of its stretches.

Which brings me to the vistas, their totalizing
effect, the page-like given of the hill's
curve against sky, on which we are written

and so passed on to the future.
The fog bank is nearer. The crickets sing
in their hiddenness — of the rowers

in galleys, shackled to decks,
their whole lives to kill unseen,
crawling with their arms across the sea

in the service of powers unknown to
them. It's time the work were
put on the table: time the table itself

were tested. I walk up the hill
where the sun lingers an hour longer,
the snake and gopher holes scattered there,

thrown in relief. I think: if I could break
the pattern, I could find the pattern.
The hilltop grasses send their long shadows waving.

Stars in Leo

Across the way, a slat-barred terrace box
juts from a glass-doored apartment
and provides the evidence of life you need:
the barbecue pit surmounting a tripod,
a canvas-sling seat, nested Parsons
tables on which no reading matter
accuses the trivia-bedeviled resident.
You're always surprised by the neighbors'
non-appearance: it forces the eye away
and up to the mountain ridge horizon
where the air takes leave of miles-
distant brush — the flat-bottomed
brush of a vacuum cleaner attachment
turned over — and becomes sky, endless
and scrubbed-out with cirrus interruptions.

It's fall. The summer-gummed mind,
clotted with incidents of its own slowing,
slowly quickens. "A long way" doesn't
matter now, nor a short way add much
by way of coda. The second hand creeps
up between one glance and the next,
expeditiously, like a compass
hypnotized by Platonic Forms
of northness, certitude, salvation
in coordinates that it means
to offer up on its egg-white plate.
Meanwhile rotating, phantasmagoric,
the revisionist watch apes the zodiac,

motioning the moments through intersections,
the stoplight being dead.

Night rises from the mountains,
and the grains of stars scatter the empty
backdrop. The hours honey their inhuman
runnels like water crowding through grass.
All is in the short run lost, converted,
dumped, erased but these pinholes like those
in Easter eggs, suggesting what color,
what never-to-be-realized nature
the mind might make.
Heraldic creatures rim the mountain
with only as much light as will
confound utter darkness.
The lion sleeps in his electric mane;
the neighbor's window comes on
behind the translucent skin of a shade.

The mountain is what it came to be
so long ago that no memory of it struggles
any longer in the nets of stars, no eye
lifts from its page to look down
the imagined corridor of its past:
no sight to take you through the rock.
A towel swings from the veranda
on a wire. You can barely make it out,
but its dim rectangle promises
an immaculate white, like an empty folio page
illumined by its own immensity
of reusable beginnings; or perhaps
only by sunlight — discriminate, dramatic —
far away in a future of hours,
as morning crosses the valley.

About the Author

David Rigsbee was born in Durham, North Carolina in 1949. He was educated at The University of North Carolina, Johns Hopkins University, Hollins College, and The University of Virginia. He has taught at colleges and universities in Maryland, New York, North Carolina, Louisiana, and Virginia. Among his awards are fellowships in poetry from The Fine Arts Work Center in Provincetown, The Djerassi Foundation, and The National Endowment for the Arts. He is the author of, most recently, *The Hopper Light* (1988) and *An Answering Music: On the Poetry of Carolyn Kizer* (1990). He lives in Blacksburg, Virginia.